WALLSEND REFLECTIONS

Jean and Ken Smith

Tyne Bridge Publishing

in association with North Tyneside Libraries

Acknowledgements

The authors wish to thank the following: Marion Coulson, Colin Finlay, Ray Grew, Barbara Heathcote, Antony Hendon, Les Hodgson, Eric Hollerton, John Hunter, Ken Hutchinson, Norman Jackson, Dick Keys, Kathleen Keys, John McConnell, Nancy Main, Ian Rae, Chris Robson, George Shepherd, Joan Smart, John Stephenson, Rev M.C.Vine, Gordon Watson, the churchwardens of St Peter's and St Luke's, and the staff of Newcastle Libraries.

Wallsend Reflections is published in association with North Tyneside Libraries, Information and Museums Service.

Published by City of Newcastle upon Tyne
Newcastle Libraries & Information Service,
Tyne Bridge Publishing, 2005

www.tynebridgepublishing.co.uk

Tyne Bridge Publishing
City Library
Princess Square
Newcastle upon Tyne
NE99 1DX

Printed by Elanders Hindson, North Tyneside

Front cover: The supertanker Esso Northumbria towers over one of the terraced streets next to the Wallsend Shipyard in 1969.

Back cover: Walking up Crow Bank towards The Green, 1950s.

Frontispiece: Photographer W. Parry of South Shields records High Street West on 21 June 1901.

Photographic acknowledgements
All photographs are from the collections of Newcastle Libraries and Information Service unless otherwise indicated.

Also by Ken Smith, published by Tyne Bridge Publishing
Emperor of Industry: Lord Armstrong of Cragside
Lost Shipyards of the Tyne (with Ron French)
Mauretania Pride of the Tyne
Stephenson Power: George and Robert Stephenson
Swan Hunter: the Pride and the Tears (with Ian Rae)
Turbinia: Charles Parsons and his Ocean Greyhound

By Dick Keys and Ken Smith:
Black Diamonds by Sea
Down Elswick Slipways
Ferry Tales: Tyne-Norway Voyages 1864-2000
From Walker to the World
Steamers at the Staiths

Contents

The Wall to the Tyne   5

Perilous Depths   7

Born at The Green   21

The Church on the Hill   28

A Flourishing High Street   37

From the Ranch to the Ritz   47

Turbines and Speed   58

Legion of the Shipyard   65

Wallsend Timeline   79

Further reading   80

Walking up Crow Bank towards The Green, the historic village centre, in the 1950s. The old Mordue family brewery dominates the scene. The buildings have now become attractive town houses.

The Wall to the Tyne

Wallsend, the place where Hadrian's Wall ends – or begins, depending on the direction you are travelling – is in many ways a very special town. A Roman fort, coal mining, shipbuilding, marine engineering and other industries combined with a village green, a beautiful dene and the impressive River Tyne, all feature in Wallsend's history and make it a place of great character and interest.

To soldiers of the Roman legions who built the 73-mile long Hadrian's Wall from Bowness-on-Solway to Wallsend in the first half of the 2nd century AD (the AD 120s) this place by the Tyne was most definitely the end of their extraordinary border fortification.

It is known that the original intention was to end the Wall at Newcastle, but it was later extended to a site on the banks of the river four miles to the east – the Wall's end. From then on, the Tyne would form a natural defensive barrier against enemies from the north. Wallsend's fort, Segedunum, is believed to have been built at about the same time as this last eastern section.

The main Wall joined the fort at the south tower of the West Gate. A further stretch of wall, sometimes called the 'branch' wall, ran from the south-east corner of the fort down to the Tyne, guarding the eastern flank from attack. The lower part of this section ran through what became Swan Hunter's shipyard and terminated at the river's edge.

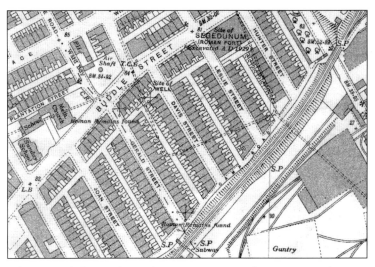

The concealed site of Segedunum in 1937, with streets stretching down to the Swan Hunter shipyard. The site has been fully excavated by Tyne & Wear Museums and reveals the remains of the fort at the end of the Roman Wall.

Segedunum – the name means 'strong' or 'victory' fort – featured an administrative headquarters at its centre, cavalry and infantry barracks, a commanding officer's house, a granary and possibly a hospital. It had five gates. Within the protective arm formed by the Wall and fort there would have been a civilian settlement nestling on the banks of the Tyne – the first Wallsend 'village'.

The Romans had first arrived at the line of the Tyne

around AD80. Their occupation lasted a long time – more than three centuries – but by c.AD 410 it was effectively over. The inhabitants of the settlement no longer had the protection of the empire and its legions.

In the 1880s terraced housing was built on top of the remains of Segedunum – with roads such as Hunter, Leslie, Davis, Gerald and Joan Street springing up over the site of the fort and its adjoining area. It seemed that the ancient stones had been lost forever under urban development and perhaps much of the site destroyed by the building work.

The housing and streets were demolished in the 1970s and happily it was discovered the site had suffered little damage. By the late 20th century the Roman fort was once again uncovered and open to the public.

A small section of the south-eastern branch wall was discovered inside Swan Hunter's shipyard in 1903 and later moved to Wallsend's Richardson Dees Park. In 1912 stones from the East Gate of the fort were also displayed in the park. Some of these remains were afterwards transferred to the public grounds of Wallsend Hall. The town's people were able to view relics of their Roman heritage in settings surrounded by flowers, trees and shrubs – but not in their original context. Fittingly, these remains have now been moved back to Segedunum; the East Gate stones now stand in their original position and the wall section now occupies a site on the line of the branch wall between the fort and riverside cycleway, as it could not be returned to the shipyard.

Now the old and the new stand side by side; Segedunum Roman Fort and Museum and a section of the main Wall foundations to the east contrast with the dramatic backdrop of Swan Hunter's towering cranes.

North Tyneside Council

Derek Henderson

Top: an old postcard shows the Roman stones in Richardson Dees Park, formerly known as Wallsend Park.

Below: Segedunum, 1994, during excavation, the cranes of Swan Hunter towering over the site. The remains of the fort at the end of the Wall can be surveyed from the museum's viewing tower.

Perilous Depths

Wallsend was once famed for its top-quality coal. Black diamonds from the rich seams below the area's streets, buildings and fields were highly valued worldwide. Large numbers of Wallsend men worked in extremely dangerous conditions to win coal and earn a living for their families, many of whom lived in the rows of pit cottages which were dotted about the district.

These early 19th century terraces, including Shiney Row, Church Pit Row and Long Row, housed families whose experiences and links of trust and friendship led to strong bonds. They also sometimes shared the ordeals of tragedy when mining accidents took the lives of men and boys in the pits, which were fraught with perils such as gas, dust, flooding and roof falls.

The era of mining in central Wallsend began in 1778 when work started on sinking a shaft – eventually known as the A Pit – a short distance west of Segedunum Roman Fort and slightly south of the fort's West Gate. This was Wallsend Colliery's first shaft.

The project to sink the pit was initially led by William Chapman, a talented engineer with an inventive frame of mind. However, problems with water and quicksand were encountered and costs mounted. Soon the scheme was in financial difficulties and Chapman and his partners were forced to hand the uncompleted shaft and coal leases over to

Thomas Hair's 1830s engraving of the 'C' or Gas Pit of Wallsend Colliery, clearly showing the piped and flared off gas, top left. 'C' Pit was one of the seven shafts of the early colliery. The pit was situated in what became Richardson Dees Park.

a creditor, William Russell senior, a merchant and financier.

Luck was on Russell's side, for the coal of the High Main seam was reached in 1781, a very short time after the unfortunate Chapman had withdrawn from the venture.

The High Main was found at a depth of 660ft and the A Pit began production. Soon afterwards another shaft – the B Pit – was sunk close by, almost immediately north of the present day Buddle Street, again a little to the west of the fort and close to the line of Hadrian's Wall. Five additional shafts were sunk between 1786 and 1802, making a total of seven. These were the C, D, E, F and G pits.

Some of these shafts acquired nicknames such as the Gas Pit for C, because gas was piped from the mine via its shaft. The gas that emerged into the air at the top of the pipe was kept alight to burn it off. The G pit was known as the Church Pit because it was not far from the town's St Peter's Church.

Another mine with a small colliery community developed in the late 18th century on the western fringes of Wallsend. The village became known as Bigges Main after landowner Thomas Bigge. The mine was abandoned in 1856 and the site of the village is today occupied by part of Wallsend Golf Course.

The 'black diamonds' won from Wallsend's High Main seam were of superb quality and fetched top prices on the world's markets. Indeed, coal from other areas was sometimes sold under the name 'Wallsend' in an attempt to make more profit.

At first using horses and the force of gravity, but later sometimes steam locomotive power, the coal was transported the short distance from the town's pits to staiths (loading jet-

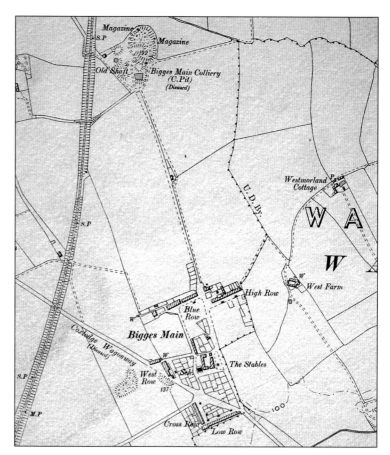

Bigges Main colliery village, and the disused pit, top, among the farms and fields just north-west of central Wallsend, from the OS map of 1898. The North East Railway snakes north, left. Today a golf course lies directly over the site of the old village.

ties) on the river's banks from where it was loaded into keels or collier ships. It was boom time for William Russell senior and his descendants, Matthew and William junior. Russell senior became a very wealthy man.

However, by 1831 the High Main was virtually exhausted

and afterwards coal was mined from another seam, the Bensham, 200ft below. The Bensham was noted to be particularly 'fiery', presenting the pitmen with the constant danger of gas.

The hazardous nature of this seam was demonstrated with appalling effect on June 18, 1835, when 102 men and boys from the town were killed as the result of a gas explosion in the mine. Many seem to have died from suffocation or the effect of gas inhalation in the aftermath of the blast. Other bodies were found with burns and crush injuries.

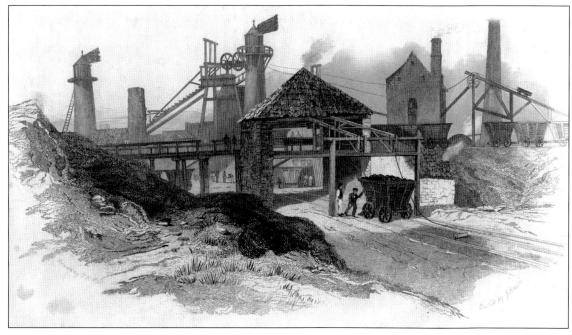

The 'G' or Church Pit of Wallsend Colliery engraved by Thomas Hair c.1830. The disaster of 1835 was centred on this shaft. Over 100 men and boys were killed in the tragedy as a result of a gas explosion.

Among the dead was an adult miner surrounded by a group of boys. The man had evidently been trying to lead the boys to safety towards the nearest shaft, the G, although had they reached it they would have found it blocked by the explosion. Poignantly, each lad was discovered with his cap in his mouth in a bid to combat the effects of the gas – the deadly 'afterdamp' of carbon monoxide which followed the blast.

Few, if any, of the rows of pitmen's cottages in Wallsend were untouched by this great tragedy. Everyone knew or was related to at least one victim. The two youngest boys killed were aged eight and nine. Several others were only 11 or 12.

The oldest miner was 76.

The dead were given a last resting place in the town's St Peter's Churchyard, not far from the G Pit site. Sadly, the grave was unmarked. There was no memorial to the miners who lost their lives.

Ironically, 39 miners who had died in the Heaton Colliery flooding disaster of 1815, were given a memorial plaque, which is still sited inside the church. They too are buried in the churchyard. Many Wallsend men and boys had worked at the Heaton mine.

It seemed illogical and unfair that the 102 who had lost their lives in the Wallsend disaster should not have a memori-

Two faces from the past, William Chapman and John Buddle.

The old Killingworth Viaduct in the Burn Closes around 1913.

al too. However, this situation was rectified in 1994 when a plaque commemorating these tragic miners was sited in the south wall of the churchyard. They had at last been given a permanent mark of remembrance denied to them so many years previously. This was made possible thanks to the efforts of Wallsend Local History Society in combination with the National Union of Mineworkers and North Tyneside Council.

During this era the viewer or manager of the colliery was John Buddle junior, a man who encouraged Sir Humphrey Davy to develop his safety lamp for pitmen and who worked on improving ventilation in mines. Buddle is also believed to have played a key role in helping William Chapman, the man who had started the sinking of the A shaft, develop some of the world's earliest steam locomotives.

The *Steam Elephant,* a locomotive almost certainly designed by Chapman, is known to have been used by the Wallsend Colliery, and was moving along wooden rails there as early as c1815-16. The *Steam Elephant* was afterwards transferred to a mine at Washington, but was then returned to the Wallsend pits where it ran on iron rails, probably much more successfully than on the wooden ones. A working replica of this engine can been seen at Beamish Museum, County Durham.

George Stephenson, the most famous steam locomotive pioneer of all, built his own iron horses not far away, at West Moor, near Killingworth. His first 'travelling engine' named *My Lord* (although some accounts say it was called *Blucher*) was constructed in 1814. He tested his locomotives on the Killingworth Colliery Waggonway.

The earliest route of this famous waggonway passed through Willington and reached staiths on the Tyne in the area which later became Cleland's shipyard. However, a later route ran down to staiths at Wallsend. This new branch of the Killingworth Waggonway passed towards the river imme-

William Chapman's locomotive, the Steam Elephant, depicted working at Wallsend Colliery. The mansion of Carville Hall is seen in the background and staiths with a coal drop, a device also designed by Chapman, are in use on the riverside. The Steam Elephant was moving along wooden rails at Wallsend as early as c1815-16. The engine was later transferred to a mine at Washington, but was returned to the Wallsend pits where it ran on iron rails. A working replica of this locomotive can be seen at Beamish Museum in County Durham. The anonymous artist has used artistic licence in this imaginary view of the geography of Wallsend.

diately to the west of the present day location of the Asda supermarket at Benton, running through part of the Rising Sun Country Park, and then veering to the south at the Rising Sun Farm, before eventually crossing the Burn Closes at Wallsend on a wooden viaduct. This viaduct was a prominent feature of the area for many years and was not demolished until c1945-46.

The track then ran past the site of the G Pit, following the line of the present day road known appropriately as Waggon Way before reaching staiths at the riverside near Davy Bank and close to the site where the North Eastern Marine Engineering works were built.

Wallsend Colliery had its own staiths and short waggonways which were connected to the various pits of the town. Horses and inclined planes were used to move the wagons and, as we have seen, locomotive power was also tried in later years.

The prized black diamonds – some bearing the name 'Russell's Wallsend' to distinguish them from 'fake' Wallsend coal – left the Tyne in the holds of small sailing colliers, many bound for London and the South-East.

The man largely responsible for sinking the town's first mine shaft, William Chapman, invented the 'drop' method of loading coal at the staiths which involved lowering a wagon onto the deck of a ship using a system of pulleys and weights. Alternatively, the black diamonds would be cascaded down a spout or chute into the vessel's hold.

Park Road follows part of the line of the wag-

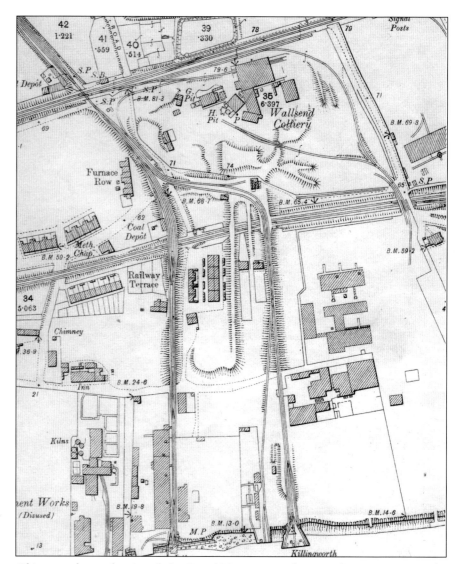

This map shows the site of the G and H pits around 1898. The site was immediately to the west of the present day Hadrian Road Metro Station. Waggonways can be seen running down to the Tyne, with Killingworth Staiths bottom right.

gonway which linked the C Pit to the staiths. These staiths were close to the Killingworth Colliery staiths in the area between North Eastern Marine and Parsons' works.

One of the most up-river of the coal routes passing through Wallsend was the Kenton and Coxlodge Waggonway, which ran down to staiths at the foot of what is now Benton Way.

In his excellent and highly detailed work, *History of the Parish of Wallsend* (1923), local historian William Richardson told of a particularly sad incident during the early days of the colliery when the coals were brought to the surface in wicker baskets known as corves. They would be attached to a chain on the end of a winding rope, three at a time. Men and boys also hung on to this chain, when corves were not attached, to take them into and out of the pit. This was, of course, a highly dangerous arrangement. It seems that none of the shafts yet had a cage to provide a much safer way of descending and ascending.

Richardson tells us: 'A boy was returning up the shaft clinging to a chain, with his older brother just below him. The youngster felt the chain slowly slipping through his hands. He called out 'I'm gannen to fall, Jimmy.' 'Slide down to me, hinny,' his brother replied. But when the boy slid down his brother could not hold him. In spite of an agonising struggle the chain slowly slipped through his fingers, and together they went to their death.' In our own health and

The 'G' pit of Wallsend Colliery after it was reopened for production in 1898. The new 'H' Pit was situated close by and within the same complex. It had opened for coal drawing the previous year. The colliery was now owned by the Wallsend and Hebburn Coal Company.

safety conscious times it seems almost unthinkable that any employer should expose boys or men to such a terrifying danger – but this was the era of the Industrial Revolution when many companies gave little thought to the safety of their workforce.

Despite the 1835 pit disaster and other tragedies involving loss of life, mining continued at Wallsend for nearly 20 more years. But by this time the colliery's profits had fallen considerably. The Bensham seam proved much less lucrative than the High Main since its coal was suitable mainly for gas

13

making, and the gas industry was at an early stage of development. With profits dwindling, William Russell junior pulled out of mining in the area towards the end of 1847. The next year new owners took over the colliery.

The first phase of 19th century mining in Wallsend came to a dramatic end which saw the town's coals absent from the market for nearly 50 years. Between 1854 and 1859 nearly all the mines of the Mid-Tyne area, both north and south of the river, were overwhelmed by floodwater and forced to close. These included Wallsend, which in 1854 was one of the first to cease production as water poured relentlessly into the tunnels. Not until 1866 did work start on reopening the colliery.

Those involved must have known that pumping the water from the mine would be an immense and lengthy task. Pumping engines were set up at the G Pit and operations began on sinking a new shaft, the H, under 100 yards away.

The pumping work lasted a long time at both the G and H shafts, but gradually the water level was greatly lowered. This helped to reduce the level in some of the other collieries in the Mid Tyne area, but Wallsend remained closed because its owners concentrated on resuming mining at Hebburn Colliery.

Coal was too valuable a commodity to waste. The Wallsend and Hebburn Coal Company was formed in 1892 and one of its aims was to restart production at Wallsend. This goal was achieved in 1897 when the first coals were drawn from the new H Pit. During the following year the G Pit started production again.

The G and H pits of the colliery were situated close together on land immediately to the west of today's Hadrian Road Metro station and immediately to the east of Waggon Way, being bordered to the north by the Metro line. (See map on page 12.) The G and H pits closed in the 1930s

In 1908 the Wallsend and Hebburn Coal Company opened another mine in the area north of the Coast Road. This was the Rising Sun Colliery, named after a local farm. Work had begun on sinking the first shaft to the Bensham seam in 1906. The mine was to become one of the largest on Tyneside and by the early 1960s around 2,000 men were employed there.

Norman Lindsay, of Wallsend, began work as a trainee surveyor at the Rising Sun Colliery at the age of 14 in 1940, but after only three months had to leave when his family moved to Shilbottle. His father had been a deputy at the Rising Sun and was taking up a similar position at the Shilbottle mine.

After serving in the Army during the Second World War, Norman rejoined the workforce of the Rising Sun in 1948, this time as a trainee pitman. He remembers Vesting Day that year when Britain's mines were officially nationalised. To mark the transfer of the Rising Sun from private to public ownership a Union Jack was flown atop the pithead winding gear.

Norman writes: 'In March 1948 after being demobbed I came to Wallsend. I decided to get a job with the Rising Sun Colliery. I had previously been employed there at the age of 14. I started work on the day shift with two marras. We were employed as timber leaders. I was very apprehensive on my first day, but my worries were unfounded. As far as my workmates were concerned I couldn't have done better.

'After entering the pithead baths I left my clean clothes in the clean locker and walked past the shower with my towel around my waist, and changed into my pit clothes on the dirty locker side. Then everyone would leave the baths to collect their lamps and identity discs. I met my marras at the shaft top and we went down together to the Three-Quarter Seam. On emerging from the cage it seemed like entering another world, and would take some time to get accustomed to.

'On the way inbye we collected our pony from the stables. He was all black and named Jackie, and we were all greatly attached to him.'

Norman was to stay at the Rising Sun for five years and comments:

The Rising Sun Colliery pithead shortly before closure in 1969. The pit had opened for production in 1913.

'Our work down the mine kept us all fit. It was a hard life but I have no regrets at having lived it that way. True friendship counted a lot, and still does, in this world. I often wonder where they all are, and I think of our times together.'

Ray Grew worked at the Rising Sun from 1964 until its closure in 1969, after which he stayed on for a while to help carry out salvage operations. He started at the age of 16 as a trainee, serving at first, like Norman, in the transport section and eventually progressing to become a fully-fledged miner at the pit face.

Ray's work in transport involved taking timber pit props and sometimes girders to the men extracting the coal. These were transported in tubs or trams, and were often pulled by the mine's numerous pit ponies, known to the men as Gallowa's (a reference to the Galloway breed of pony).

There were two working seams in the Rising Sun at this time, the Brockwell and Beaumont, and each had its own underground stables for the ponies. The two stables were whitewashed and included an area for grooming. Each stable housed around 30 ponies. Every one of these magnificent little animals had its own stall. They spent most of their lives underground but were sometimes brought to the surface.

'I remember the ponies sometimes being brought up from the pit and taken to stables above ground on the site of the Edward Pit, which was in the area where the Tyne Metropolitan College building at Battle Hill is today,' says Ray. The Edward Pit was an old one which had reopened for production in 1913. This area was used as a training ground for the animals.

In August 1925 the Edward Pit was hit by tragedy when five miners, two under the age of 20, were killed as a result of an explosion. It was thought that the blast was caused by a spark from a coal-cutting machine coming into contact with unexpected gas.

The ponies pulled the tubs carrying the props and girders during Ray's time at the Rising Sun, although until the early 1960s they were also used to haul coal.

Norman Lindsay says that many people believed that the pit ponies were blind but this was untrue. They were able to see, but when brought to the surface their eyes took a little while to adjust to the light.

For many years the Rising Sun had two shafts, No 1 and No 2. In the early 1960s a third shaft was sunk, very much

Ray Grew

Miners pose for a picture on the surface at the Rising Sun in the 1960s. They are wearing kneepads and their traditional 'hoggers' (shorts).

wider than the other two and around 1,200ft to 1,300ft deep. The No 3 was used to draw the coals to the surface. By this time No 1 was used mainly for ventilation and No 2 (around the same depth as No. 3) for the men. The deepest seam being worked at this time was the Brockwell, reaching a depth of perhaps 1,400ft. The coal was taken away from the pit by trains.

'The Rising Sun was a fairly gaseous mine,' says Ray, 'and in its south-east and south-west sections it was wet. In the south-east area there were roadways which might contain water up to six inches deep and water leaked from the roofs. In some places the effect was like a bathroom shower! To the north conditions were much drier.'

Ray points out that some of these roadways ran beneath Wallsend High Street. 'In fact, there are mine tunnels under much of the town.'

It was possible for a miner to go on an underground walk from the Rising Sun workings to the tunnels of the old G Pit, a distance of around two miles. Ray sometimes did this walk when he worked in the ventilation section. There were said to be about 50 miles of tunnels beneath the area.

The closed G Pit might no longer have been producing coal but for many years its shaft was used for ventilation. A pumping station was also installed at the bottom of the shaft to keep the water levels down in the Rising Sun workings. The old pit cage and wheel were still in place to enable maintenance to be carried out. As well as walking along the underground roadways to this area, Ray also sometimes descended the G shaft in the cage.

From near the bottom of this shaft one of the tunnels sloped downwards towards the river. Ray noted that on old colliery maps it was marked as the 'Hebburn Roadway'. He explored this tunnel but found that after 50 to 100 yards a dam blocked any further progress. It was holding back water. Did this roadway once lead under the Tyne to link up with the workings of Hebburn Colliery? We do not know the answer, but it is an intriguing question.

The gas in the mine was methane and Ray remembers many times seeing the flashes of light that indicated its presence as he worked at the coal face with a shearer machine. He recalls that a pumping station man at the G Pit was killed by an explosion in the early 1960s.

Danger was ever present. Ray tells of a man being killed by a roof collapse while working at the face in the Brockwell seam only a few months before the closure of the Rising Sun in April 1969. He also remembers a fatal accident with a shearer machine a few years earlier.

Colin Finlay, of the High Farm Estate, also lives near the colliery site. He worked at the mine for around five years,

George Shepherd collection

Miners became very attached to their pit ponies. Here a group in the transport section show off their 'gallowa's'.

starting as a trainee in 1955 at the age of 15. He remembers the camaraderie between the men. 'We were always singing. The song with the words "You load 16 tons" was particularly popular. We would sing down the mine and as we were being drawn up and down the shaft in the cage.'

Colin also tells of the water in some parts of the workings; the Brockwell seam in particular was noted for its dampness. 'I've seen men doubled up, half submerged in water as they shovelled the coal,' he says. The Rising Sun had a reputation as a hot pit. 'It was very warm. Men would often work in just their shorts, which were known as hoggers.'

Indeed, it was so warm that on one occasion Ray Grew and some of his fellow miners fell asleep while on night shift. When they did not appear at bank a search party was sent out for them. They were discovered safe and well, but they had been asleep for several hours!

Not far from where Ray lives is the Welfare Field, off Kings Road North, where the miners played football and other sports. It is opposite the former colliery entrance at the top of the road. Colin Finlay recollects the annual sports day attended by the miners and their families which sometimes featured pit pony races.

The field was also used for whippet racing. This was very popular and the nearby workingmen's club, The Barking Dog (whippets don't bark!), was often full of these dogs and their owners. The whippet racing took place regularly on Sunday mornings but gradually declined after the Rising Sun closed. In 2005 The Barking Dog is still a popular pub.

With the colliery's demise a way of life which had lasted for two centuries vanished, although smoke still seeped from the coaly ground above the mine for many years afterwards, a reminder of even more coaly times past. The site of the Rising Sun Colliery became a country park, managed by North Tyneside Council. Three slag or spoil heaps which once dominated the scene have been landscaped and remodelled into two pleasant hills, the highest known as Rising Sun Hill. Now there are only memories of the time when men toiled underground to win the black diamonds from Wallsend's perilous depths.

The Rising Sun colliery workings, top right, are still prominent looking west along the Coast Road c.1960. Central is Wallsend Technical College, which became North Tyneside College, and was renamed Tyne Metropolitan College in 2005.

The college area was also the site of Edward Pit, opened in 1913. Opposite the college was Battle Hill House, built c.1914 for Charles A. Nelson, a mining engineer working with the three Wallsend pits. In the foreground, right, are the miners' cottages of Embleton Avenue. The houses on the left are in Gibson Street.

In the late 1960s the whole of the Coast Road was rebuilt, opening in 1969. The photograph was taken from the 14-storey Willington Farm Estate flats, opened 4 November 1960. Highly desirable at the time, the flats have since been demolished.

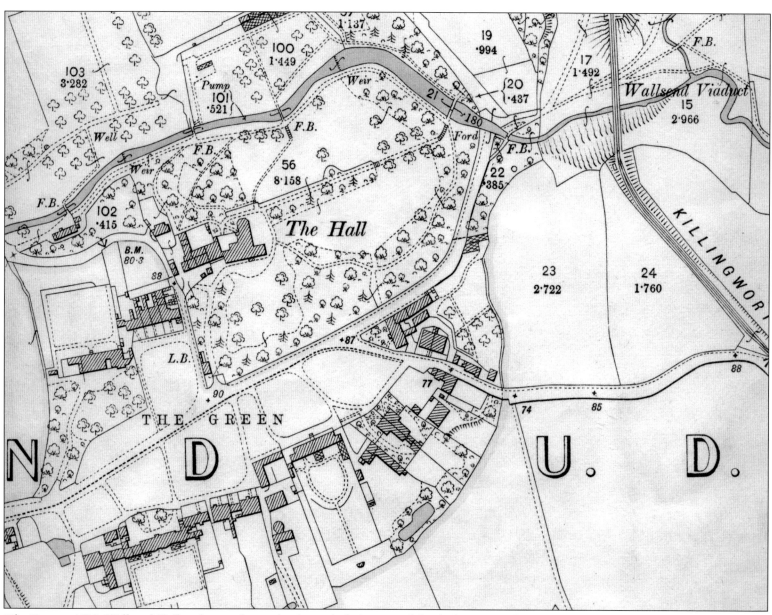

The Green c.1898. Wallsend Hall and grounds are clearly marked. Crow Bank leads down past the Hall grounds to the Burn Closes and the Killingworth Waggonway, with its viaduct, far right.

Born at The Green

Wallsend Village Green is a delight to encounter unexpectedly in a town so normally associated with heavy industry. Situated about one mile from the Tyne, The Green dates back for hundreds of years. It had developed as a new settlement to the north of the Wall some time after the departure of the Romans. In early times it had even been a place of punishment – there were stocks on the area's western edge.

In the 19th century The Green area was a typical English village, built on a square. It featured a mansion, large houses, cottages, a vicarage, a school house and farmsteads. The Green was also used as a meeting place and for entertainment.

The Green, looking east towards Crow Bank on the far left, around 1890. In the background far left is the old school house. The tall property next to the school house is Dene House which was built by the Mordue family. Even at this date it has a rural air.

Wallsend Hall around 1930. It is believed by some to date from the early 19th century, although no one seems completely certain of the exact date. The foundations may be even earlier.

By the opening years of the 20th century the area had started to change. Some of the big houses were demolished and more modest villas built. New schools were opened elsewhere. Some of the large houses which remained were changed from homes or country retreats of the wealthy into community buildings.

The imposing mansion of Wallsend Hall still stands on the north side of The Green, and it seems at least one earlier Hall occupied more or less the same spot. The Hall has had many owners and occupiers, who were often prominent citizens of Wallsend. Some had large houses in Newcastle and the Hall was their out of town retreat.

The present building is believed by one leading architectural historian to date from the early 19th century, but nobody seems certain of the exact date. What is certain is that alterations were carried out to the property in Victorian times.

In 1856 Robert Richardson Dees, a wealthy solicitor, purchased the Hall. In 1897 he gave some of the land he owned nearby to the town to create Wallsend Park. This pleasant, green recreational area was later named Richardson Dees Park. The shaft of the old C or Gas pit of Wallsend Colliery was in what is now the park's south-eastern corner, close to the tennis courts.

Robert Richardson Dees died in 1908 after living in the house for over 50 years. This prominent lawyer was a bachelor and the property was left to his nephew Robert Irwin Dees. He had modernisation work carried out at the Hall and moved in with his family in 1909. They stayed only a few years and left the house in 1912, selling it to Wallsend shipbuilder Sir George Burton Hunter in 1914. Hunter presented the Hall and most of its grounds to the borough council in 1916.

During the First World War the house was used to accommodate Army officers stationed in Wallsend. Later, part of the building became the Civic Hall. The mayor gave tea parties there and it is still the venue for many functions.

The rest of the Hall became a small hospital, which included a maternity department. Many people living in and around Wallsend will tell you they were 'born at The Green'. The medical and maternity part of the Hall was known as the Hunter Memorial Hospital (later the Sir G.B. Hunter Memorial Hospital). At the time of writing it is used as a hospital and day centre, but the maternity department has closed.

A modern mother and baby centre known as the Sunray Clinic was built next to the Hall. This was completed in 1940 and was part of a government scheme to provide model up-

The Civic (Wallsend) Hall grounds c.1950s.

to-date facilities for mothers and young children. The building is still used by the local community health trust.

The small road leading down hill between the clinic and the next buildings to the east is Crow Bank, and is well-known to Wallsenders. This led to the village pump and Holy Cross Church on the other side of the Burn Closes. It is said that cows could often be seen wandering from one or other of The Green's farmsteads down Crow Bank to drink in the burn below, a rural scene which seemed remote from the town's industrial activities.

Wallsend Hall, left, and the Sunray Clinic, right, in 1951. Many Wallsend residents will remember as children receiving sunray treatment for the prevention of rickets (goggles would be worn).

Fronting the road on the east side of The Green and facing west was the village school and schoolhouse. Previous owners of the Hall had given the schoolroom, schoolhouse and garden to the parish in 1748. It was used as a school until 1835.

Between 1790 and 1808 the schoolroom was even pressed into service as a makeshift church. Marriages and christenings took place. Robert Stephenson, son of George, the railway pioneer, was baptised there in 1803. He had been born at nearby Willington Quay.

However, the idyllic setting of the school did not mean that things were always peaceful. The building became the subject of an ownership dispute with the parish. The Mordue family had been schoolmasters since 1776 and were allowed to rent the property after the school closed. However, by 1893 it was discovered that the family had not paid any rent.

Francis (Frank) Mordue had built two very large semi-detached houses in the schoolhouse garden. Dene House is one of these properties. He also managed a brewery attached to the back of the schoolroom facing on to Crow Bank. It seems the parish had left it too late and the Mordues had acquired squatters' rights. The buildings have changed very little since those times. The present day Mordue Brewery, based in North Tyneside, is named after the family.

Across Boyd Road, on the south side of The Green, is the

site once occupied by the old vicarage. This had a small front garden and a large orchard at the back. The property was sold to George Auburn Allan in 1880 and he built a new house in the orchard and demolished the old vicarage. A farmhouse and other buildings next door were pulled down in 1875. The land was sold to the Hall farm estate and Robert Richardson Dees built two semi-detached villas on the site. These are East and West Villas.

Opposite the Hall was a large house called The Grange. It was last occupied by two brothers, William and John Russell. They were the owners of Walker Copper Works. John committed suicide in the garden in 1883, and perhaps unsurprisingly William moved out of the house shortly afterwards.

On William's death in 1893 The Grange was sold to a Gateshead auctioneer and estate agent who in turn sold it to Robert Richardson Dees. The house with a tragic story was later demolished and Grange Villas erected on the site in 1913.

The Village Farm made up the next group of buildings on the south side. This ceased to be a farm in 1881 and the land was finally sold to the Battle Hill Estate Company in 1921.

Another property fronting the south side of The Green was the White House. This had large pleasure grounds which included a fish pond and a shrubbery as well as a kitchen garden. The house, and 11 acres of land, were bought by a Thomas Chater in around 1838. He let it out to various tenants. Chater also built The Villa on the east side of the house. A Mrs Thomas Stewart was the last owner of The White House and occupied the property until 1903. The

Victorian ladies pose for this idyllic picture in front of the old school and house. The Mordue brewery is to the rear of the house on the left. This photograph is from W. Richardson's History of Wallsend.

house was then pulled down and became the site of a skating rink.

On the same side of The Green as the Hall, and opposite the White House, was the Red House. This was a three-storied mansion built in red brick. It had over 20 rooms and two acres of land with gardens and stables. Robert Richardson Dees also acquired this property in 1882. It became a home for children with disabilities in 1889 and was equipped with 50 beds. The home moved to Gosforth in 1897.

Afterwards, the Red House was demolished and Hawthorn Villas built on the site. Park Villas were put up in part of the garden. A site between the Red House and the Hall had been occupied by Village North Farm. This was replaced by Elm Terrace in the 1870s.

Wallsend Village Green was also used as a social gathering place and was often a bustling and lively area of the town.

Marion Coulson was born at The Green. She lived with her parents at Deneholme, Holy Cross and remembers Easter gatherings on The Green on Good Fridays in the 1950s.

'You would meet at your church, then join the queues marching to The Green. If you didn't have a church you would join any queue. All the churches had their banners and civic dignitaries would come. You always had new clothes.

'We used to go to the Allen (Memorial Church) for an apple and orange. The lads would sometimes join on the end of the queue again to get a second lot.' They would joke to the boys: 'You'll get caught'.

Many people went to the park on Easter Sunday 'and met on The Green for a natter. Then we went to roll our paste eggs down the burn'.

The Green would often be used on special occasions and 'there would be children's egg and spoon and sack races. People walked to the park across The Green and you often met someone you knew. Children would take a picnic on The Green during the school holidays'.

Marion's father worked in the shipyards as a charge hand electrician. He would walk backwards and forwards to work from Holy Cross via The Green. 'We would meet him on The Green after walking up Crow Bank'. He worked long hours in the yards, often doing overtime and must have been tired on the walk home.

Joan Smart, née Dixon, was also born at The Green. She lived in Frank Street, Wallsend, and remembers the gatherings at Easter.

'The shipyard band would play. The Boys' and Girls' Brigades, Scouts and Guides and Sunday schools used to come. There would be a church service and the children would get an orange and apple. We would sing *There is a green hill far away* and other Easter songs. We had new socks and sandals and sometimes a bonnet. All our family used to go to my Gran's for home-made fish and chips'.

The park is used for more varied activities now including the Easter gatherings. The Green is quieter. It has been designated a conservation area and has new signs, railings and seats. But this beautiful location still has the character of a classic village green and is a little oasis of countryside in the town, a surprise to visitors who have heard of Wallsend's history of coal, ships and engines.

Right, the Easter Hoppings funfair at the Burn Closes in the 1950s. On the skyline is the large crane of Wallsend Slipway and Engineering on the banks of the river. On the left in the distance is Willington Viaduct. Haggie's Rope Works is the low dark building top left. The works were founded c.1789. Robert Hood Haggie took over Willington Ropery c.1840. Much of the old works was destroyed by fire in 1873. However, the premises were rebuilt and the business continued as a family run firm.

The Church on the Hill

The earliest known church serving Wallsend village was Holy Cross, founded c.1150 on a small hill above the shallow valley of the Burn Closes. To the east of The Green it was reached via Crow Bank. A paved 'church way' led from the village across the Wallsend Burn to the churchyard steps which climbed the hill. Coffins were carried along this path, which must have seemed very long to the bearers.

A hearse road led from Willington village but only the well-off would be brought to the church this way. As well as funerals, the church was used for marriages, baptisms and private prayer, but rarely for ordinary services, until the late 1700s when it fell into disrepair. Marriages and baptisms were then held in the schoolroom at The Green.

In 1797 William Clarke, who was living at Wallsend Hall, decided to renew the roof of Holy Cross. The old one was taken down, but Clarke then moved away from the district and left the church open to the skies. This hastened the decay, and walls, some gravestones and railings were broken up or taken away. The church and churchyard fell into ruins.

By 1909 the church was so ruinous that the churchwardens had the interior cleared of rubbish and the walls preserved with cement. Railings were erected around the churchyard, removed during the Second World War, and since replaced. The ruins of Holy Cross still stand starkly on the hill as a reminder of medieval times in the Wallsend district.

The ruins of Holy Cross around 1900.

Holy Cross had been the only place of worship between North Shields and Newcastle and with its demise a new church was urgently needed. A meeting was held in 1791 in order to decide whether to rebuild or enlarge the existing church. It was agreed to rebuild the church to hold 500 people.

But for more than 15 years, meetings, discussions and Acts of Parliament (read and dismissed) took place, still with no new church in sight. It appears money was the main problem compounded by the fact that no one wanted to take responsibility for the project.

It almost came to court when the Bishop, Dean and Chapter of Durham threatened the churchwardens with legal action to make them repair Holy Cross. Still nothing was done, until it was discovered that the schoolhouse was unconsecrated and not licensed for marriages.

It was an extraordinary revelation that must have sent shock waves through the community. Marriages which had taken place there were illegal and any children born to those couples were illegitimate. In those days it was regarded as an enormous scandal. Indeed, the matter caused such upset and anger that, at last, an Act of Parliament was passed in 1807 to sanction a new church on a site at the top of what is now Church Bank.

The Act legalised the banns and marriages performed in the schoolhouse thus legitimising the children. The new legis-

Holy Cross Church around 1909 with repairs underway.

lation also authorised the raising of money.

The foundation stone of St Peter's Church was finally laid in 1807. The new church was quite plain at first with a square tower and a 'candle snuffer' shaped spire. There were large square pews, some of which were reserved for the leading landowners and residents of large houses in the parish.

However, it seemed that not everyone wanted to go to the new church. A pair of stocks was installed in the churchyard to punish Sabbath breakers. *The Northumberland Advertiser* reported on 18 September 1832 that two young men, who had been playing games on a Sunday morning, were placed in the stocks for two hours 'to their complete shame and confusion'. The other 'disorderlies' were known to the police and would be put before the magistrate if they did not 'desist from their Sabbath breaking pursuits'.

The churchwardens of St Peter's also had to deal with young men gathering around the church door before and after the service. Watching the girls maybe? This caused 'great annoyance to many frequenters of public worship'. The stocks are still in the churchyard.

In 1892 extensive alterations were made to the church, including the removal of the spire.

At some time in the past the font of Holy Cross had been found in the Wallsend Burn and in 1891 this relic of the old church was given to St Peter's by Neptune Yard shipbuilder John Wigham Richardson. The interior also features 14 carved wooden angels, reminiscent of ships' figureheads, high above the pews on each side of the nave. They may have been carved by a shipwright – this would certainly be appropriate for Wallsend's strong association with ships and the sea.

Memorials inside St Peter's include a stained glass window given by the Cripples' Home to thank the people of Wallsend for the kindness shown to them during their two-year stay in the Red House on The Green.

The manager of Swan Hunter's Wallsend Shipyard during the building of the great passenger liner *Mauretania* was Christopher Stephenson, who died aged 53 in 1912. He had attended St Peter's and a brass plaque memorial to him was installed in the building by the directors and workers of Swan's. Another window was provided in 1922 by Christopher's widow, Margaret, to the memory of two of her children, Robert and Sylvia, who died during the First World

St Peter's Church shortly after the alterations of 1892.

War. This window, two others also on the north side, and two in the vestry are made from beautifully crafted Irish glass.

The population of Wallsend increased rapidly in the late 1880s as its industries grew. It became apparent that a new church was needed in the western part of the town.

The parish of St Peter's was divided in 1887 and the western area became St Luke's parish. The land for the new church, on the corner of Station Road and Frank Street, was donated by shipbuilder George Burton Hunter. The foundation stone was laid in 1885 and St Luke's was consecrated in 1887. The first vicar stayed for about five years and was replaced by the Rev W.M. O'Brady Jones in 1892.

Just two years later tragedy struck. To raise funds for the building of the church's vestries, children of leading families in the town were to provide an evening's entertainment

CHURCH BANK, WALLSEND-ON-TYNE

Church Bank, before 1910. St Peter's Church and Wallsend Cemetery are top left. Beyond the cemetery is the churchyard, where the 102 victims of the 1835 mining disaster are buried. The road crosses Willington Gut, and Burn Closes is to the right. The Rose public house was built in the foreground in 1913. Since 1720 there has been a Rose pub in this area. The Tynemouth to Newcastle coach made a regular stop at the inn where extra horses could be attached to help with the long haul up Church Bank, or up Rosehill Bank on the other side. One of the earlier buildings was used as a Catholic church in the mid-19th century when there was nowhere else for local Catholics to worship.

during Easter 1894. The Rev O'Brady Jones' daughter, Kathleen, aged 11, was to play two violin solos. The rehearsals took place at the Co-operative Hall in Carville Road. However, the actual entertainment was never staged. The *Newcastle Daily Chronicle* reported the next day on a 'Shocking Affair at Wallsend.'

The paper declared: 'The quiet town of Wallsend was thrown into a state of great excitement about 5 o'clock yesterday afternoon by a report that Miss K. O'Brady Jones had been accidentally shot in the Co-operative Hall. The young lady having been shot through the temples by a bullet from a revolver.'

It appears that 'several lads who were allowed to be present had with them a revolver. The weapon was taken from them, and on examination was found to be unloaded'.

The boys gathered round the front entrance as the entertainers left the building. Suddenly there was the sound of a shot and young Kathleen collapsed. Doctor Henry Aitchison was summoned, but by the time he arrived Kathleen was dead.

At the inquest at the Wallsend Café in Station Road, Robert Anderson, aged 14, said he had bought the gun in the

St Luke's c.1900. On the right is the vestries building which was dedicated to Kathleen O'Brady Jones.

SHOCKING AFFAIR AT WALLSEND.

A CLERGYMAN'S DAUGHTER SHOT DEAD.

The headline in the Newcastle Daily Chronicle on 29 March 1894.

Bigg Market, Newcastle, the previous Wednesday and had used it for shooting practice. He could not remember if he had loaded it in the hall. His friend, John Dewar, aged 15, had been playing with the revolver and snapping the trigger. As people were leaving the hall, John pointed the gun at Kathleen and it went off. The jury and coroner concluded that Kathleen's death was accidental.

John Dewar was charged with 'causing death' and remanded in custody. He was brought before the county magistrates but discharged as the Bench agreed the shooting was undoubtedly an accident and thought that John would be punished enough by having to live the rest of his life knowing that he had been the cause of Kathleen's death. They also said they would 'make representation to Her Majesty's Government regarding the sale of firearms to young persons'.

Kathleen's funeral was held on Easter Saturday, March 31, 1894, and her coffin was carried to Wallsend cemetery by members of St Luke's Choir. The roads from St Luke's were lined with people paying their respects to the tragic little girl.

The vestries at the west end of the church were eventually built and dedicated to Kathleen's memory in 1895. A stone tablet in the outer vestry records the story of her death.

In 1906 the chancel, Lady Chapel and a tower of 140 feet were completed. The plans included a spire and bells but the ground under the foundations was unsuitable. The fine, large east window of stained Irish glass, unveiled in 1922 is a memorial to 269 men of the parish who died in the armed forces during the First World War. A brass tablet records their names.

St Luke's is known as the 'Shipyard Church' and was well supported by George Burton Hunter, who headed the

North Tyneside Council

The O'Brady Jones family shortly after the tragedy.

Wallsend Shipyard for many years.

St Columba's Roman Catholic Church began as a mission chapel and school which opened in 1876. Many of the people who came to work in the colliery and shipyards were from Ireland and Scotland and this increased the need for a Roman Catholic church.

In 1904 a large timber-framed building with a corrugated metal roof (nicknamed 'the tin cathedral') was built between Chadwick Street and Carville Road to serve the Catholic population. This could seat 700 people. It was replaced by the present St Columba's Church which was consecrated in 1957.

A considerable number of Methodists lived in Wallsend. A site in the Carville area on the western side of the town had been used on the Methodist preaching circuit from about 1802. It seemed logical to build a meeting place near to this spot and in 1812 the Carville Chapel was opened near the A and B pit shafts. It stood between Buddle Street and Plantation Street and appropriately became known as the 'Colliery' Chapel. A new chapel was built on nearby land and opened in 1906. This building was across the site of the Roman Wall. The old chapel became a Sunday School and was also used for youth meetings.

As part of the Coronation Celebrations

Above: St Columba's Church c.1930. Below: the 1957 St Columba's under construction.

for King George VI in 1937 a rock garden was opened in the Carville Chapel grounds by Irene Ward, MP for Wallsend. The central rockery was made of Roman Wall stones from the demolished Stotts House Farm nearby.

Joan Smart was married at the Colliery Chapel in 1973. She had also attended Carville School nearby. She remembers the school's Empire Day celebrations. 'I used to wear my Brownie's uniform. We would sing Rule Britannia and There'll Always Be An England and wave a flag'.

Carville Chapel was eventually demolished along with the surrounding houses. Excavations have taken place on the chapel's site and a large portion of the Hadrian's Wall foundations can now be seen, as well as the remains of the nearby B pit. A replica of a section of the Wall is also on display in this area.

When some members of the Carville Chapel left to set up the breakaway Methodist New Connexion in 1835 it took some time for them to acquire a new church. A site and a large subscription were eventually donated by local businessman John Allen, a wealthy chemical manufacturer and the foundation stone was laid in 1857 on the north-east corner of Station Road and the High Street. The building was used until 1903 when it was sold. A new church was opened in 1904 in North Road and in recognition of John Allen and his wife it was named the Allen Memorial Church.

Today, less people attend church and the population of

The old and new Carville 'Colliery' Chapels around 1912, from a booklet celebrating the centenary of Carville Chapel. The old chapel is on the left.

Wallsend has shifted further from the town centre area. The result has been that the two Anglican parishes of St Peter's and St Luke's are once again united, sharing a minister and services.

The Allen Memorial Church in North Road around 1908. The children and prams are in Wallsend Park, opened in 1900 on the site of C Pit, Wallsend Colliery. The terraced houses on North Road had not long been built, in fact one is awaiting its upstairs windows. By the 1980s the spire of the church had to be removed as it had become unsafe.

A Flourishing High Street

The main part of the town is centred on the High Street, which is divided into two sections – east and west – by Station Road. In the early 1900s the shops lining this busy thoroughfare were flourishing as the heavy industries of the district boomed.

On High Street East stands the grand Town Hall, which was opened in 1908 to accommodate the new Wallsend Borough Council formed in 1901. The building has a round tower on its western corner and a clock that was started up as part of the opening ceremony. The Town Hall is now the headquarters of North Tyneside Council.

A boom town like Wallsend needed services. The first bank opened in what is now High Street West in 1890. In the early 1900s the North Eastern Bank moved into an imposing building

The Town Hall, left, around 1950, looking down High Street East towards Station Road.

on the north west corner of Station Road. Martins Bank later took over the building.

You could buy just about whatever you wanted in Wallsend. There were at least four fish and chip shops as well as butchers, fruiterers, fishmongers, confectioners (some confectioners were also bakers) and several pawn brokers. Pringles, the confectioner must have been a successful business. It is listed in directories for 1913 and was still there 30 years later. Grocers included Greenwells, on the corner of Hedley Street, and W. Wilson's in High Street West, Home and Colonial Stores and Liptons were in High Street East.

High Street West around 1900. The Ship Hotel is on the right, with its clock high above the street.

If you were looking for clothes you could try Burtons store, the 'gentlemen's tailor and outfitters' which was opposite Martins bank beneath the windows of the Wallsend Café. On High Street East there was Bon Marché 'drapers and latterly ladies outfitter'. For hats you could try the millinery shop in High Street East, and for stockings Tinkler the hosier on the same street, another business which survived for at least 30 years. If you needed a boot and leather shop you were spoilt for choice. Directories for 1913 list 14 in the High Street, including a saddler. For medicines and toiletries there was Boots the Chemist which opened in the Central Building on the old site of the New Connexion Church, or independent chemist W. Giles.

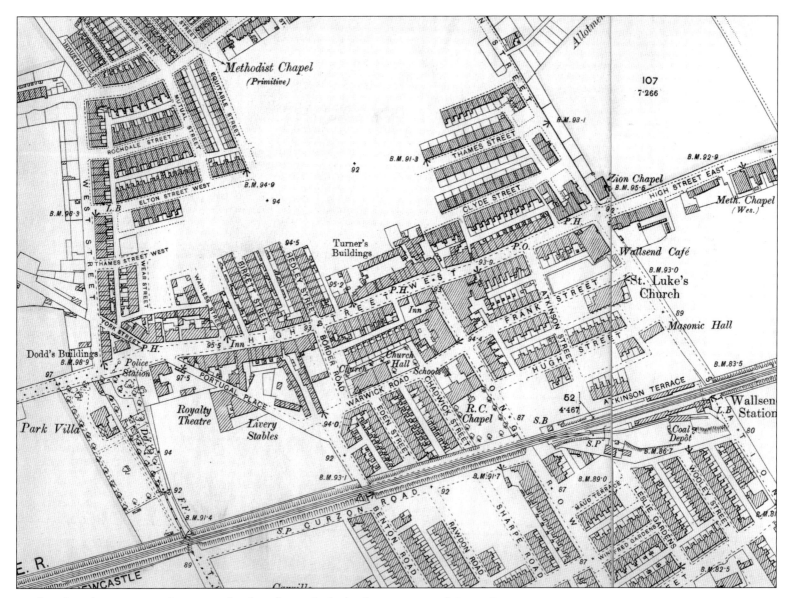

Wallsend High Street around 1898. At this date there is little development in High Street East.

North Tyneside Council

Tyler's pit boot shop (reliable goods low price) in High Street West around 1896. The young boy is Frederick White. Next door was Giles the chemist.

C. Fisk, butcher and H. Thomson, fishmonger and game dealer, ply their trade around 1910. Rabbits made a good, cheap meal.

High Street West, Wallsend's most prominent thoroughfare, bustles with life in 1911. Tram lines run down the middle.

HIGH STREET EAST, WALLSEND.

202769.J.V.

A view around 1930 from the Station Road crossroads looking towards High Street East. Boots is on the left and the curved building in the distance is the Borough Theatre beyond the Brunswick Church. The building on the far right was Burton's the tailors, beneath the Wallsend Café.

Many people have fond memories of shopping at the Co-op and the shop belonging to the Wallsend Industrial Co-operative Society Ltd was one of the town's largest businesses. The society had started in 1862 with two rooms converted into a shop in Carville Road (then Long Row). A window and a door, wide enough to allow a cask of sugar to be rolled in, were made to front on to the High Street. The shop sold general grocery goods.

The Co-op became so successful that the shop continued to expand down both sides of Carville Road until it reached Frank Street and Warwick Street. The arch on Warwick Street used to lead to the Co-op stables. You

The Co-op on the corner of High Street and Carville Road from a 'History and Handbook' published by the Wallsend Industrial Co-operative Society in 1912.

can still see two plaques on the shop's Carville Road frontage. The one on the left depicts a beehive with bees. On the right is a plaque with joined hands, a Co-operative Movement symbol. The Co-op Hall was in this building.

Following its expansion the Co-op store had departments for hardware, confectionery, a fruit shop, a dairy, a tailor, dressmaking, millinery and a very successful cobblers. It had its own slaughterhouse reached through the rear entrance in Warwick Street. It seems the stables were eventually moved to the second floor of the new building, though it is hard to

imagine how they got the horses up there!

Many of the High Street's shops survived the First World War and the depression of the 1930s. Some changed hands and sold different goods, but the street was essentially the same. During the 1950s and 60s, when work was plentiful, the shops thrived and expanded.

Joan Smart remembers the Co-op. 'You could buy almost anything there'. She also recalls seeing the horses and carts going in and out of the stables in Warwick Street.

Marion Coulson recollects the furniture department and

jewellers which were added to the store after the Second World War. She sometimes went to the Co-op's grocery section for her Mam who always said to her: 'Don't forget to bring my cheque back'. The 'cheque' was the dividend record which grew with each purchase and could be redeemed quarterly for a share of the Society's profits. Wallsend Store had a reputation for the biggest dividend in the region.

Assistants at the Co-op did not use cash registers. Instead, a system of overhead wires and canisters carried money to and from the cashier's office.

A Woolworth's store opened opposite the Co-op in High Street West. Watson's the leather shop was a little closer to Station Road. They sold all types of leather – from whole hides to hard pieces cut to sole and heel shoes. Other stock included hob nails, rubber and steel tips, studs for tap dancing shoes and clogs, and laces that were cut to the required size from a long strip of leather. Pitmen knew this store well – Watson's was probably the only shop in the town that sold miners' soft leather hats and knee-pads.

Marchis ice cream parlour and coffee shop opened in High Street West before the First World War and was still trading in the 1950s. It had long tables and bench seats. Joan Smart would meet her friends there. 'We used to sit on the bench seats and as more people you knew turned up you would get squashed up. I would have an ice cream sundae, you know a knickerbocker glory. I wasn't into coffee, but now and again I'd have one. We would sit there for ages'.

By the 1970s the High Street was changing. Some of the older shops had been demolished and a new shopping centre, The Forum, had been built in the 1960s. Several High Street retailers, including Boots and Bon Marché, moved there.

Looking west towards High Street West in the late 1950s. Above Books (Fashions) Ltd. are the tall windows of the Wallsend Café. The building, which was funded by George Burton Hunter, also included meeting rooms and classrooms. It was the first building in Wallsend to be lit by electric light. In 1925 the splendid Wallsend Memorial Hall, with a sprung dance floor, was constructed next door in Frank Street (see page 77), and the buildings were connected.

Woolworth's relocated to the corner of Station Road, and the Co-op built new premises in Station Road which were linked into The Forum.

High Street and Station Road were not just for shopping as Marion Coulson remembers: 'If there was a launch people would congregate on Station Road and the High Street to see the Queen or whoever was coming to launch the ship'.

Marion worked at Swan Hunter's Wallsend Shipyard for 34 years. She started as a junior secretary in the Swan's pensions office, then moved to the registrars and finally spent 11 years in the security office. She recalls the time when she was asked to present a bouquet at a launch – the girl who was originally going to carry out the presentation had changed her mind at the last minute. 'I was asked by my boss if I could do a favour. When he told me what it was my first reaction was to say "I'll have to go home to wash my hair". He said that if they could get me an appointment at the hairdresser's, would I do it? Of course I said yes.'

Marion had to decide what she would be wearing so that her clothes did not clash with the outfit worn by Lady Jackson, wife of the British Rail chairman, who was to launch the vessel.

'I said I had a green suit and a leopard skin fake fur coat. They said "That's OK, Lady Jackson will have a real fur coat". When she arrived we didn't have time to get into place properly and she whipped off her fur coat and left it in the car. It was a bit embarrassing with me in a fur coat and her

Wallsenders relax outside The Forum shopping centre around 1970. It was refurbished in the 1990s.

not, even if it was fake.'

The eventual run-down and closure of large sections of Wallsend's heavy industry meant that smaller shops found it hard to survive. In the past people had only occasionally needed to leave the town to do their shopping, but with the advent of the Metro they began to travel to Newcastle city centre more often. Increased car ownership enabled people to reach out-of-town supermarkets and shopping complexes such as Silverlink and the MetroCentre. Despite this, the High Street and Forum can still be busy on Fridays and Saturdays, but the heyday of visiting favourite small shops seems to have passed.

From the Ranch to the Ritz

If you wanted a good night out you could head for the High Street with its pubs, theatre and later the cinema. One of the earliest public houses in High Street East was the Coach and Horses. The old building was on the Turnpike Road between North Shields and Newcastle. The present pub is a large, ornate, imposing building, dating from 1902. It stands next to the Town Hall and seems to have been the only pub at the east end of the High Street.

Before the First World War High Street West had a better choice of pubs. Moving westward from Station Road on the southern side were the Ship Hotel with its prominent clock high above the street, the Jolly Sailor and the Queens Head Inn. These three pubs, and many others in the town, were owned by R. Deuchar Ltd. The last on this side was the Anchor Inn.

The Coach and Horses, High Street East c.1900.

Across the High Street was the Duke of York, still standing today. Then, looking back towards Station Road, came the Robin Hood, the Black Bull, the Railway Inn and the Station Hotel. This last pub was known to almost everyone as the 'Penny Wet'. It earned its nickname because shipyard workers would use it for a liquid breakfast. The pub opened at 6.30 in the morning and sold coffee and rum for a penny.

Norman Lindsay, who worked at the Rising Sun Colliery, often dropped in for a drink there with his fellow miners. 'Some of us met at night time. One of our favourite pubs was the Station Hotel, known as the Penny Wet, and many a good time we had in the bar alongside the shipyard workers. The favourite quote was 'You can't hear with the noise of ships being built, or see for coal dust'.'

Two vanished Wallsend pubs, left, the Station Hotel, or the 'Penny Wet', 1960, and, right, the Jolly Sailor, 1967.

By the 1940s and 50s, all of these pubs were still trading but some of the smaller houses had been taken over by Newcastle Breweries including The Anchor, Railway and Station Hotels. The Blue Star was now a familiar sight in the town.

The Station Hotel was demolished when The Forum was built and was replaced by The Anson which is still known as the Penny Wet.

The Black Bull and the Railway are no longer open. The Jolly Sailor and the original Ship are gone; the latter was demolished in the 1980s and a bank built in its place. The Queen's Head still exists but the Anchor is now Jimmy's and the Robin Hood has been renamed The Ship.

Of course there were other public houses away from the

The Anchor Hotel, 1965.

North Tyneside Council © M. Dunn

The Davy Inn, 1966.

High Street. Two worth remembering are on the edge of the town. The New Winning is almost opposite St Peter's Church, at the top of Church Bank. The present building dates from 1894 but the first pub on the site was probably named after the sinking of the G pit and the 'winning' of its first coals.

The Davy Inn was near the Tyne foreshore, down what is now Davy Bank and below Railway Terrace. This pub was associated with the Mordue family who brewed beer at the back of the schoolhouse on The Green. It was used by men working at the North Eastern Marine Engineering works and Wallsend Slipway and Engineering.

Gordon Watson, who worked at Wallsend Slipway & Engineering, sometimes visited the Davy Inn with his friends to play cards. The bar had many mementoes left by visiting seamen. 'I particularly remember a small pair of boxing gloves and it seemed that a seaman who played a game of snooker had taken his collar off. He left the cue he had used and the collar behind the bar.' This was a common thing for seamen to do in the belief it would ensure a safe return from their voyages.

Of course, not everyone drank and there were several temperance clubs and societies in town. These included George Burton Hunter's Wallsend Café in Station Road, near its junction with the High Street. Close by was a Temperance Cycling Club. The Co-op and the Café ran libraries and reading rooms. In 1913, Marchis ice cream parlour was listed in directories as a temperance bar.

In 1910 a skating rink was opened on the White House site between The Green and North View. The

The Ship Inn next to the Wallsend Shipyard, 1966.

Wallsend Herald and Advertiser's headline read 'Grand Skating Rink, Wallsend. The largest in the North.' It described the entrance 'from North View and there are five emergency exits. There is a commodious café upon one side of the rink and the orchestra will be accommodated upon the balcony. In addition to these are the usual cloakrooms, ladies' retiring rooms, skate rooms, offices and a kitchen for the use of the staff'. Of course, there was no piped music! A cinematograph room was also provided and the premises were 'lighted throughout by electricity' – a favourite boast of the early 1900s when electric lighting was at the forefront of technology.

- - A GRAND - -
Exhibition
OF
CO=OPERATIVE ..
... PRODUCTIONS

From July 13th to 20th, 1912,
Will be held in the

Olympic Skating Rink,
WALLSEND-ON-TYNE.

Opening Ceremony
On
Saturday, July 13th, at 3 p.m.,
By
HIS WORSHIP, THE MAYOR of WALLSEND,
Ald. Jas. Allan, J.P.

Chairman :
COUN. THOS. G. HUNTER,
President of the Society.

Speakers :
C.C. JOS. ENGLISH, J.P.,
Birtley, (C.W.S. Director) and
JOS. WARWICK, ESQ.,
North Shields, (C.W.S. Director).

Wallsend Herald advertises the Co-op jubilee at the skating rink in 1912.

The Stadium, as the old skating rink had come to be known, before its demolition in June 1986.

In 1911 the Rink hosted a fancy dress skating party, followed by a confetti battle. In 1912 an exhibition to celebrate the Co-op Jubilee was held there. However the Rink did not flourish. During the war years of 1914-18 the building was used to construct aircraft.

The Shields Daily News reported that a boxing tournament was held at the rink 'in aid of the wounded soldiers in the Royal Infirmary, Newcastle'. Soldiers and men from Wallsend took part in the competition and exhibition bouts. After some time as a boxing hall, it was taken over by Daimler in 1922 and used as a car factory.

From 1926 until the 1940s the building served as a Ministry of Labour Training Centre and later was used by the DHSS. It was demolished in 1986 and new housing built on the site. Part of the development is called Stadium Villas.

The Borough Theatre in High Street East opened in 1909 and staged numerous variety shows and pantomimes. The large curved building with a small wrought iron balcony above the entrance and ornately carved auditorium must have been impressive in its heyday. It stands out prominently from the surrounding buildings as you look down High Street East from the Station Road junction. The tickets sold at the theatre were made from brass – a good example of recycling! The theatre eventually became a cinema, then a bingo hall and now houses an amusement arcade.

In the 1950s there was a dance studio on the upper floor above the cinema. Marion Coulson was taken there for lessons. 'Mum would drop me off at the door and then go shopping in the High Street. It was tap dancing and ballroom and I hated it. I used to skip off to the park. I knew the time she would be back and I would be sitting on the stairs waiting for her. Of

Alexandra Rose Day is celebrated with a parade on High Street West after 1909. Queen Alexandra was very popular and associated with many charities. The large building on the right of the street flying a flag is the Wallsend Café. The Borough Theatre is in the distance on High Street East.

course, she found me out. The studio sent a letter home for a contribution for a show and she asked me what I was dancing, and of course I couldn't tell her'.

Norman Jackson was born at home in Leslie Street near

Simmons Aerofilms

The impressive facade of the Borough Theatre stands out prominently in this aerial view of High Street East and its surroundings photographed 27 October 1927. The church on the left is the Brunswick Church which dated to c.1901. Opposite Brunswick Church is the old church, by this time the Royal Cinema.

the Swan's shipyard. At the age of four he had his first trip to a Saturday matinée for children. 'The noise was terrific and I remember turning round and getting hit in the eye with some orange peel.'

This didn't put him off going to the pictures however and in the mid-1940s Norman went to the cinema about three times a week, depending on how much pocket money he had. There was plenty of choice. The Borough Theatre was now the Gaumont cinema. Braidford's music and record shop occupied the lower part of the building and Norman would buy 78 rpm records there.

On the opposite side of the street was the Royal. This was nicknamed the 'Ranch' as it showed mainly cowboy films. 'It would get so rowdy that the manager would stand on the front seats with a cane and hit the seat (sending up a cloud of dust) to get the audience, mainly boys, to quieten down.'

Round the corner in Station Road opposite Frank Street was the Queens. Norman was friends with the manager's son. 'I used to be able to get in free. It had an open ceiling with iron girders. We used to go upstairs and if you sat in the wrong seats you had to lean your chin on the girder to see the film.' The building is now a shop but the front and shape of the entrance are still recognisably a cinema.

Across the High Street, still in Station Road, was the Tyne. This is where Norman saw his first film. In the 1950s the Tyne was renamed La Continental and showed adult films in a last ditch attempt to stay open. The Anson public house now occupies the site.

Looking west along High Street West in the 1960s. The Ritz is on the right of the street.

The poshest cinema in Wallsend was aptly named the Ritz. It was in High Street West next door to the Black Bull. It opened 15 May 1939. Norman recalls: 'The Ritz had a lovely entrance floor of Italian tiles and red plush seats and was decorated in the Art Deco style. There was an undercover area to queue outside and after the war they opened a sweet shop inside that was very popular after rationing stopped.' The Ritz was hit in a bombing raid during the war and the foyer was damaged.

The Ritz in 1939, the year it was opened. Some of the original features of this fine art deco style cinema were still retained when it became a bingo hall.

McDonald's Pictures on Station Road is thought to have been the first purpose-built cinema on Tyneside. Opened in 1909 it became the King's from 1913 until 1921, when it was renamed the Queen's. It closed in 1961 and later became a fireplace showroom.

Norman became a monitor of the ABC Minors Club at the Ritz. On club days they would show mainly serials. 'The monitors would meet with the manager and have tea and buns and be told where they would be and what would be showing. We had a badge and an armband and would be given a couple of rows to look after to make sure they behaved themselves or they would get turned out. Of course we would get to see the film for free'. The Ritz building is still in the High Street and is now a bingo hall.

Wallsend Park was the place for outdoor amusements. Laid out on land given to the town by Robert Richardson Dees in 1897, it included bowling greens and a bandstand. Later came tennis courts. It is now named Richardson Dees Park in memory of its benefactor. Wallsend Dene and the public grounds of the Hall were ideal for strolls and the Burn Closes has been used for recreation by generations of Wallsenders. This shallow valley leading down to the Tyne at Willington Quay is still a large, green space in the middle of the North Tyneside conurbation.

During the 20th century residents and workers in Wallsend were able to find plenty of ways to use what leisure time they had in the town. But as fashions changed and people became more mobile they travelled further afield for the cinema, theatres, pubs and clubs in places like Newcastle city centre and the coast.

A corner of Wallsend Park near the main entrance c. 1900. It was later renamed Richardson Dees Park.

A group of men in their Sunday best pose for a picture at allotments in Wallsend in the early 1900s. Growing vegetables and flowers on allotments has been a strong tradition in the North-East. The man holding the flowers is Richard Patterson, grandfather of Nancy Main. Born on Holy Island, his first job at Wallsend was to look after the horses at Haggie's Ropeworks, Willington Quay. Haggie's employed large numbers of women and was a leading business in the area. Richard Patterson later went into business as a carter.

Turbines and Speed

Marine engineering had the lowest profile of Wallsend's industries, perhaps because shipbuilding, with its spectacular launches and impressive vessels, had always stolen the limelight.

Despite the unromantic nature of their exacting and complex work, Wallsend Slipway & Engineering, North Eastern Marine and Parsons Marine had a reputation for providing first-class propelling machinery and boilers for ships of all kinds. These three Wallsend firms, with their frontages on the river, played a leading role in establishing the Tyne as one of the most important marine engineering centres in Britain.

The trio of companies occupied sites close to one another, the most westerly and furthest up river being the Parsons Marine Steam Turbine Company, which was set up in 1897 by Sir Charles Parsons to develop and manufacture his invention, the marine steam turbine engine for propelling ships at high speeds.

The company opened the Turbinia Works on the riverfront at the bottom of Davy Bank, slightly down river from the Swan Hunter shipyard, in 1898. Parsons had already founded the Heaton Works in Newcastle for the manufacture of land-based electricity-generating turbines in 1889.

The famous steam yacht *Turbinia* was the first vessel in the world to be driven by steam turbine machinery. The revolutionary boat, nearly 104ft long but with a beam of only 9ft, was designed by Parsons and his team and built at Wallsend by Brown & Hood, a sheet metal firm. *Turbinia* was launched from the Brown & Hood works fronting the Tyne in 1894. The vessel was constructed of extremely thin, light steel to help her achieve high speeds.

This extraordinary boat sailed on her trials in the North Sea from moorings at Wallsend, with Sir Charles usually at the controls in the engine room. These test runs were vital for the development of the invention.

At the Review of the Fleet in the Spithead anchorage off Portsmouth in 1897 the long, sleek *Turbinia* dashed between the lines of moored warships at what was then an astonishing speed of 34.5 knots, equal to nearly 40 land miles per

Turbinia on a trial run off Jarrow Slake in her early years.

hour. This was a brilliant publicity stunt for the turbine and it was not long before the Admiralty began ordering engines for its ships.

Only a short distance down river from Parsons were the works of North Eastern Marine Engineering, often known simply as NEM. This company had originated in Sunderland and opened its yard and factory at Wallsend in 1882. The early 1900s saw the business become one of the first in the town to switch entirely to electric power. A large electric cantilever crane, said to be the first on the North-East coast, was installed on the firm's quayside in 1909. It was capable of lifting up to 150 tons and quickly established itself as a familiar landmark of the Tyne.

A similar large crane was operated by the Wallsend Slipway & Engineering Company, immediately down river to the east, adjoining the premises of NEM.

The heavy-lift crane in operation at the NEM quayside between the two world wars. Photograph by W. Parry of South Shields.

'The Slipway', as the firm became known, built the turbine engines for such mighty vessels as the Swan Hunter-built passenger liner *Mauretania*, completed in 1907.

The company also provided the turbine machinery for the battleships HMS *Queen Elizabeth*, HMS *Malaya*, HMS *King George V* and HMS *Anson*, the last three of these being launched on the Tyne. The *Anson* was completed during the Second World War at Swan Hunter's Wallsend Yard.

The Slipway site, now occupied by the mothballed yard of offshore technology company AMEC, featured huge sheds, and the large electric crane on the Tyne quayside, capable of lifting up to 180 tons. NEM and the Slipway used their giant cranes to lift heavy engines and boilers into ships moored alongside their yards. Many of these vessels had been built on the river.

Engineering had not been the original aim of the Slipway's founders. The company was formed in 1871 solely for the purpose of ship repair, acquiring a site fronting the Tyne and bordered on its eastern edge by the entrance to

Willington Gut. Two slipways around 1,000ft long were installed to accommodate ships in need of repair or maintenance. The company began operations in 1873 with the repair of the *Earl Percy*, which belonged to the Tyne Steam Shipping Company. This steamship served on the Newcastle-London route carrying passengers and goods.

The following year William Boyd became managing director, and it was he who began developing the engineering side of the business which was to become so important in

Wallsend Slipway and Engineering Company works in 1920, photographed from an airship. This picture is from a promotional brochure published in 1921.

later years. The first engine produced, of only 120hp, was completed in around 1875-76, and greater developments were to come.

In 1878 Wallsend Slipway & Engineering constructed the first steel boiler to be produced on the Tyne. In 1882 another milestone was reached when it produced the river's first triple expansion engines. These were fitted into the cargo steamer *Isle of Dursey*.

In 1896 Andrew Laing, a brilliant engineer from Edinburgh, began work as manager at the Slipway and was

soon reorganising and enlarging the works so that it could provide engines and boilers for the largest vessels. The Tyne-built Russian icebreaker *Yermack* was one of the first in a long line of major ships to be engined by the company under Laing's direction.

William Boyd and Andrew Laing also paid a great deal of attention to the use of oil as a fuel. Laing, who eventually became general manager and a director of the business, developed a successful system to enable oil to be used efficiently for marine boilers. The company went on to produce oil-burning units for many vessels.

Wallsend Slipway & Engineering also gained a good reputation for its production of quadruple expansion engines, installing them in ships such as the Swan Hunter-built Cunard passenger liner *Carpathia*, which rescued the survivors of the *Titanic* disaster in 1912.

But the company was perhaps most famous for constructing turbine propelling machinery, starting with the Newcastle-owned vessel *Immingham* in c1905-06. A much

Part of the jetties area at Wallsend Slipway and Engineering, showing dismantled machinery and boilers awaiting shipment c.1920.

greater development came shortly afterwards. The powerful engines of the *Mauretania*, the Tyne's most famous ship, were perhaps the company's greatest achievement. This represented a personal triumph for Andrew Laing and his team since turbine engines of such power had never before been installed in a ship. Although Sir Charles Parsons had developed the principles of the marine steam turbine engine, it was Laing and his colleagues at the Slipway who designed and constructed the extraordinary propelling machinery for the record-breaking liner.

Mauretania was completed at Swan Hunter & Wigham Richardson's Wallsend Yard in 1907. Generating 68,000hp, her turbine machinery put in splendid service and ensured the liner held the Blue Riband for the fastest North Atlantic crossing for a record 22 years on the eastward passage and 20 years on the westward. She regularly notched up 25 or 26 knots on her voyages between Liverpool or Southampton and New York.

During the First World War the Slipway was clearly kept at full stretch. It provided machinery for 68 vessels and a further 151 vessels were repaired.

In the early 1920s the company declared: 'Employment is given to a veritable army of men and boys, comprising shipwrights, boiler-makers, fitters, blacksmiths, moulders, pattern-makers and representatives of all other skilled handicrafts associated with marine engineering and naval construction.'

A workshop at the Slipway during World War I with women workers much in evidence.

John McConnell, originally from Willington Quay and now living in Battle Hill, served his time as an apprentice fitter at Wallsend Slipway & Engineering during World War II, starting in 1940, and remembers the big crane well. His grandfather, Jack Turner, and great grandfather, Willie Turner, also worked for the company. Grandfather Jack, who lived at nearby Willington Quay, was a chargehand fitter on the *Mauretania* contract and did not retire until he was 80. 'It was my grandfather who helped me get started at the Slipway. He worked there for 66 years.'

John tells of a vast shed which housed several departments, including the workshop where precision blades were processed for the turbines. This shed, the one nearest the road, also housed sections including the fitting, erection and machine shops. John worked in the fitting shop – always known as the 'top shop' – on items such as valves for Howdon patent oil-burning units needed for ships' boilers. The demand for these units gave the company a great deal of business. When John first started his employment with the company the workforce was finishing off the job of fitting machinery for the aircraft carrier HMS *Victorious*, which was to take part in the operation against the German battleship *Bismark*. The demands of wartime kept the Slipway extremely busy. He recalls the yard was generally working on building and installing three sets of turbine engines at the same time. 'They were normally just starting work on one set of machinery, one set was half finished and one ready for installation.'

John also remembers the 540ft-long dry dock where repairs to ships were carried out – the company was still in this business despite its huge engineering interests. As well as repairs, some vessels were docked for what was known as a 'haircut and shave', which meant painting and cleaning, or for other maintenance work. The dock had been built in 1895, but by the time John joined the company the two early slipways had long since vanished – they were dismantled in c1909-1910.

John watched the 180-ton crane in action many times. It had a maximum reach of 140ft. 'The company also had a coal-fired steam crane on the quayside which ran on lines.' He points out that ships could berth alongside the yard in the entrance to Willington Gut as well as at the company's main quay fronting the Tyne.

Sometimes John was seconded by the Slipway to Swan's Wallsend Shipyard to carry out work. It was during one such spell that he narrowly avoided an accident. He and a fellow apprentice were re-boarding the aircraft carrier HMS *Vengeance* after the dinner hour and were taken up the side of the ship by a lift. However, by mistake they got out of the lift a long way from their work station and decided to take a short-cut across a wooden plank positioned at a great height.

'What we didn't realise was that the plank was warped. My friend decided to go first, but when the lad got to the middle of the plank it began wobbling. He dropped to his knees and crawled the rest of the way.' Understandably, John did not attempt to follow his workmate and decided to walk the long way round. The two men are still friends.

He also recalls playing in the Slipway apprentices' football team and the 'brilliant' canteen at the works. John left the Slipway in 1946 to join the Royal Navy, but eventually returned to work for the company for another two years. By this time the Slipway's products included Doxford patent diesel engines which were in great demand from shipping companies. Afterwards, he joined the Merchant Navy.

A Wallsend Slipway and Engineering workman with a turbine for HMS Furious.

Gordon Watson, from the Kings Estate, began work as an office boy in the drawing office of Wallsend Slipway & Engineering at the age of 15 in 1952. Joining the company was something of a family tradition – three of his four brothers and a sister also worked there. His sister was employed in the tracing shop.

Gordon served his apprenticeship as a fitter at the Slipway from 1953 to 1958 and was in the first group of apprentices to enter the company's newly-formed training school. During this time, he worked on lathes, milling machinery, drilling and with hand tools.

He went on to carry out such tasks as assembling valves and also served in the bearings section which involved 'strenuous and demanding' work on turbines. In addition, he sailed on the trials of three ships engined by the company, two of them tankers. It was clearly a varied life.

Gordon agrees with John McConnell over the 'excellent' workers' canteen at the Slipway – the meals had such a good reputation that employees from other yards often went there. The canteen featured a stage for social functions and at least one episode of the popular radio programme *Workers' Playtime* was broadcast from there.

In 1958, Gordon left Wallsend Slipway & Engineering to join the Merchant Navy, but after four years at sea he 'came ashore' and – like John – went back to the Slipway for a two-year spell.

It seems the company was regarded as a particularly good

The 180-ton crane towers above the quay at Wallsend Slipway in 1946.

employer. During the late 1950s it was employing around 3,000 people and a considerable number of these stayed for many years. For example, in June 1959 the company, then part of the Swan Hunter Group, held a presentation ceremony for those who had given 30 or more years of service to the Slipway. A total of 338 people, including five women, were presented with watches – it was an impressive number by any standards.

Legion of the Shipyard

The streets were filled with men on foot. They came from all directions. There was the clatter of boots and shoes on the pavement and roadway as an army of workers made their way down Swan's Bank into the famed Wallsend Shipyard in time for the 7.30am start. Then, when the buzzer went for the dinner hour at 12 noon, men who lived in the town rushed up the bank on their way home for their mid-day meals prepared by their wives or hurried into the canteen just outside the yard gates.

Finally, when the buzzer marked the end of the main working day, this same army surged through the gates bound for home, some men running. A vast crowd – laughing, talking, animated but tired after their labours building sturdy queens of the seas, ships destined for owners worldwide.

That daily inrush and outrush of the shipbuilding 'legion' at Swan Hunter's Wallsend Yard was one of the most impressive sights of the town.

Sprinkled among the crowd were the women workers. They made an important contribution to Swan's efforts. During the Second World War women were employed tacking together ships' plates in preparation for welding and some assisted the riveters. Also during the war, the company set up a shell-making shop which mainly employed women. In peacetime, a considerable number worked as tracers in the drawing office and as cleaners, which involved boarding ships under construction.

Swan Hunter workers pour up Station Road after a shift c.1960.

Some workers came from south of the river, journeying every day on the Hebburn-Wallsend ferry which had a landing next to the yard at the bottom of Benton Way. Others arrived on foot from the streets of Wallsend, Walker and Willington or by bicycle and car.

If they were coming from the direction of Newcastle or the coast, they might use the Riverside Branch railway which ran past the yard, alighting at Carville Station on Hadrian Road. From there, the workmen had only a short walk to reach Swan's.

They would also arrive by electric train on the line between Newcastle and Tynemouth, getting off at Wallsend Station, now on the Metro line, and walking along Station Road and down the bank. Others would arrive by tram, and when these were phased out, by trolley bus.

To many people the name Wallsend conjures up images of towering cranes criss-crossing the Tyne skyline, hulls tak-

Swan Hunter workmen and boys c.1909. The lad sitting cross-legged on the right, Robert Curry of Wallsend, was still working at the company nearly 50 years later and had become a foreman.

ing shape on the building berths and launch days with enthusiastic crowds watching another ship enter the river. Anyone arriving by Metro at Wallsend Station from Newcastle cannot fail to be impressed by the new Swan Hunter company's array of large cranes, including the giant red ones which can been seen for miles around.

Mrs Nancy Main

The Wallsend Shipyard produced one of the greatest passenger liners of the early 20th century, Cunard's illustrious *Mauretania*. This ship became a potent symbol of all that was best in Tyneside workmanship. Many people in Wallsend and the rest of Tyneside still look back on the liner with immense pride. She was a speed queen upon the North Atlantic. Built in Wallsend and engined in Wallsend, the *Mauretania* was a sea-going ambassador for both the town and the river.

Mauretania leaves the Tyne for her preliminary trials in the North Sea in September 1907. Tynemouth Priory can be seen in the distance on the right. The ship became a symbol of all that was best in Tyneside workmanship.

However, the great liner was not the only such floating envoy of Swan's skills. Over a period of 130 years a procession of fine ships has entered the Tyne from the Wallsend Yard's slipways – passenger liners, cargo-passenger liners, cargo ships, ferries, oil tankers, cruisers, destroyers and aircraft carriers have all been launched from the yard. Swan Hunter forged for itself a reputation which placed the business in the premier league of world shipbuilders.

The company which was to grow into such a successful business began life in a modest way in 1874 when Charles Sheriton Swan senior, who had been managing director of Wallsend Slipway & Engineering, was appointed by his brother-in-law Charles Mitchell to manage a shipyard at Wallsend which had run into financial difficulties. The yard had been run by two of Mitchell's business associates, Coulson & Cook.

The new business formed to operate the yard and hopefully rescue it from its problems was appropriately named C.S. Swan & Company. Swan's Wallsend Shipyard was born.

Tragedy was to intervene in 1879 when the hard-working Swan was killed in a paddle steamer accident in the English

Channel. He had been returning from a business trip to Russia with his wife and was leaning over the side of the vessel when he fell and was hit by one of the paddles.

The untimely death of the shipyard's leading man was a considerable blow. However, a new 'captain' took over the helm at the Wallsend Yard. He was George Burton Hunter, a shipbuilder from Sunderland, who became the managing director after entering into business partnership with Charles Sheriton Swan's widow, Mary. In 1880 the company was renamed C.S. Swan and Hunter.

George Burton Hunter went on to become one of the great benefactors of Wallsend. He was instrumental in giving land at the Burn Closes to Wallsend Borough Council for the enjoyment of the town's people. Shortly before the First World War he bought Wallsend Hall on The Green and, as we have seen in an earlier chapter, gave this historic house and much of its grounds to the borough. The Hall became the Hunter Memorial Hospital.

A fervent teetotaler and advocate of temperance, he played a leading role in 1883 in establishing the Wallsend Café in Station Road bordering the south-west corner of its junction with the High Street (see map on page 39). This extraordinary establishment served food and non-alcoholic drinks and provided rooms for clubs and trade union meetings, a lecture hall, classrooms and a games room. Technical education was delivered in the classrooms.

Hunter was Mayor of the borough in 1902-03 and clearly took a keen interest in the community. But it was as the industrious head of the Wallsend Shipyard that he became best known. Under his direction this great shipbuilding base went from strength to strength. In 1884-1885, the yard built its first two steel ships, the Australian vessels *Burrumbeet* and *Corangamite*. The use of iron was soon phased out.

Another milestone in the company's history occurred in 1903 when it merged with the shipbuilding business of John Wigham Richardson, who operated the Neptune Yard at Low Walker, Newcastle. One of the reasons for the amalgamation was to bid for the order to build the *Mauretania*.

The merger between the two companies was to prove permanent and brought the Wallsend and Neptune yards together in a highly successful association on the north bank of the river under the name Swan Hunter & Wigham Richardson Ltd.

In the same year the new business took over the shiprepair facilities of the Tyne Pontoons & Dry Dock Company, situated between the two yards. This became Swan's dry dock department. Swan Hunter & Wigham Richardson now commanded a very long river frontage opposite Hebburn.

The decade before the First World War was the heyday of the two yards in terms of orders won and completed. In 1906 and 1912 they held the world record for gross tonnage of shipping constructed. In 1907 their output of ships totalled 15 per cent of the world's total tonnage built in that year.

Mauretania was not the only vessel keeping the company occupied in 1907. The Wallsend and Neptune yards were engaged on building no less than 11 other ships that year. All were merchant vessels. At Wallsend work was proceeding on a pair of cargo-passenger liners, a North Sea passenger ferry and two cargo ships.

Between them, the Wallsend and Neptune yards produced more than 1,600 vessels. Swan's list of customers was truly

An aerial view of Swan Hunter's Wallsend Shipyard in 1970. People living in the terraced houses at the top of the picture could go down to the bottom of their streets and look over the shipyard wall to see the launches. Large vessels such as supertankers would loom over the streets. The Ship Inn is at the top of the picture, just left of centre. A supertanker takes shape on the building berth.

international, with orders received from a host of countries, including Britain, France, Portugal, Spain, Italy, Sweden, Canada, Norway and Japan.

During the Second World War, the Wallsend Yard output even included a battleship, HMS *Anson* (a public house in the town centre is named after her). She was a sister of the famous Walker-built *King George V*. The *Anson* was delivered in 1942 and one of her main roles was to provide back-up cover for the Russian convoys.

Swan's was a leading builder of oil tankers, and the company was at the forefront of tanker design until the mid-1970s. Not least of these vessels were eight supertankers of around 250,000 deadweight tonnes, completed in the early 1970s. These were the largest vessels to be produced on the Tyne.

The first of these metal giants, *Esso Northumbria*, is well remembered by the people of Tyneside. Thousands turned out for the ship's launch at the Wallsend Yard by Princess Anne in 1969 – and thousands also thronged the river's banks when she left the Tyne for delivery the next year.

While on the building berth the colossal shapes of the supertankers overshadowed nearby terraced houses in Hunter Street, Leslie Street and Davis Street. Indeed, during their construction, families in some of these homes received payments from Swan's towards their electricity bills because they had their lights on much of the time. However, these Wallsenders, and those in adjoining roads, were particularly lucky in having a grand view of launches.

One little girl who lived in Davis Street, built above the Roman fort site, until she was eight, remembered people going down to the bottom of the street and looking over the Riverside Railway wall in Camp Road to see the launches. 'As I was only young the wall seemed very high to me ... Some people stood on chairs to get a better view. Our house was only three doors up from Camp Road. I remember seeing ships taking shape and the noise from the yard as the men worked. There was a great deal of clanging. The noise often went on night and day. I recall being in bed and hearing all this shipyard activity.'

When Davis Street and the adjoining roads were demolished in the 1970s many of the families who lived there were moved to the Battle Hill and Hadrian Park estates.

Simpson's Hotel, or hostel as it was sometimes called, stood on a corner of Hunter and Buddle streets, where a large residence known as Carville House (not to be confused

Simpsons Hotel is advertised in the early 1960s.

A view down Leslie Gardens towards the Wallsend shipyard in 1970 with Simpson's Hotel on the left standing on the corner of Buddle Road. A supertanker is under construction on the building berth. Swan Hunter built a total of eight supertankers.

with Carville Hall) once stood. The hotel had been built around 1912 to accommodate workmen brought into the yards and factories on a temporary basis. Its bar had swing doors which reminded people of those seen in cowboy films and so it was nicknamed 'The Pondarosa'. The hotel enjoyed particularly superb views of launches.

Those launches included numerous cargo and cargo-passenger ships which were another mainstay of Swan's order books, with 30 being delivered for the British India Steam Navigation Company, 24 for the Ellerman Line and 22 for the Port Line.

Swan Hunter has a fine record of building passenger ships even laying aside the achievements of the legendary *Mauretania*. A notable example was the Italian liner *Giulio Cesare*, delivered in 1921 but wrecked during an Allied bombing raid near Trieste in 1944. She featured elegant interiors and luxurious accommodation as well as an impressive external profile.

Also of note was the *Bergensfjord*, launched in 1955 as

The Wallsend-Hebburn ferry landing, c.1912, with the ferry Hebburn alongside. Dominating the top of the picture is one of Swan's floating docks. This one was bound for Caleo in Peru.

the flagship of the Norwegian-America Line and delivered a year later. She had an extensive aluminium superstructure which was unusual at that date and provided a floating showcase for Scandinavian artists who contributed works for her interiors.

The list of famous ships launched at Wallsend includes the passenger liner *Carpathia*, which braved icebergs to rescue the survivors of the *Titanic* disaster in 1912; the passenger-cargo liner *Dominion Monarch*, the largest diesel motor-driven ship in the world when completed in 1939 for service between Britain and New Zealand; and the modern day aircraft carriers HMS *Ark Royal* and HMS *Illustrious*, completed in the 1980s.

In addition, more than 80 destroyers passed down Swan's slipways, most of them at Wallsend. Some fought at the Battle of Jutland in 1916 and others served with distinction during the Second World War. Among the larger warships built were many cruisers, including HMS *Edinburgh*, completed in 1939 and sunk with a cargo of gold during the Russian Arctic convoys in 1942.

The Wallsend Yard was also well-known for its production of floating docks. The company built a floating dock for the Admiralty which was moored at Jarrow Slake during the First World War and handled numerous warships damaged in battle.

In 1927 Swan's completed a floating dock for Singapore. This was towed to its destination in seven sections by Dutch tugs and provided a facility for the refit of British battleships in the Far East.

A few years later, in 1931, the Wallsend Yard completed

A 1938 snapshot, from an unusual angle, records the launch of the Dominion Monarch.

the Jubilee Floating Dock. It was towed all the way to New Zealand from the Tyne, again by Dutch tugs. At 14,000 nautical miles, this remains one of the longest tows on record.

The 20th century witnessed the changeover from riveting to welding in the shipbuilding industry. Swan's was one of the pioneers of welding and the company launched its first vessel with an all-welded hull, the *Peter G. Campbell*, as early as 1933. She was a 179ft-long barge designed for carrying oil in bulk on the Great Lakes and canals of Canada. This craft was also the first all-welded vessel built on the Tyne. After the Second World War, riveting was gradually phased out and welding became the norm.

Ian Rae lived on Tyneside for many years and worked for over 30 years at Swan's. His grandfather, Thomas Rae, like many Scots and Irish, came to work on Tyneside in the second half of the 19th century. He was from a small village close to Dalbeattie in Kirkcudbrightshire, Scotland, and was in his late 20s in 1891 when he married Ada Douglas of North Shields and set up home in Wallsend. Within six years three children were born to them.

In the 1901 census they are listed as living in the town's Park Road. Thomas found work at Swan's and was employed in the general stores. He rose to become head foreman in what was a very busy department. When they grew up, two of his children, Douglas (Dougie) and Elsie, joined their father at the Wallsend Yard in the stores department.

The Depression gripped the Tyne yards in the early 1930s, but in the later years of the decade they once again became hives of great activity as the Second World War loomed. Double shifts were worked at Swan's, which meant that peo-

A supertanker on the stocks at the Wallsend Yard in c.1971. The massive hull looms over the Wallsend-Hebburn ferry landing at the bottom of Benton Way. Even at this late date the ferry was still an important cross-river route for workers. It closed in 1986.

ple living in the nearby houses got little peace at night because of the noise from riveters.

Dougie was to follow in his father's footsteps and became head foreman storekeeper. He married during the war and Ian, his son, was born at The Green hospital in 1945.

Ian writes: 'On leaving school at the age of 16 I sat an entrance examination to be a draughtsman at Swan's. There was an intake of eight lads that year. The apprenticeship lasted five years. My first pay packet contained the princely sum of £3.10s.6d.

'The apprenticeship consisted of two years in the drawing office school, followed by three years working in the various drawing office departments for several months at a time learning about the different aspects of building a ship, including design, structural, outfit, piping, sections etc, as well as time in the actual yard with the various trades, learning how the ship was assembled.

'During this time an apprentice was expected to attend night school on three evenings a week to gain the qualifications.' By the time Ian Rae's apprenticeship had ended his wage had risen to £21 a week.

Ian adds: 'At this stage it was decided which department you were best suited for and you were considered to be a journeyman, but you had to work another nine years before

Newcastle Chronicle & Journal Ltd.

A view of the Wallsend Yard in 1983. A decade later the old company of Swan Hunter collapsed, leading to large-scale redundancies. The Ship in the Hole pub, now the Ship Inn, is just over the wall.

you got the full draughtsman's wage.' The drawing office at this time in his career had around 300 draughtsmen and women split into 'squads' of up to eight people concentrating on their own specialities. As they became more proficient, some would become 'leading hands' or even section leaders. A few rose to higher positions in the company.

Ian comments: 'The office was a cheery place with good camaraderie amongst the staff. People built up good working relationships over the years. Like all large families there were the inevitable squabbles with the company at the time of the annual wage negotiations, but common sense ruled in the end.

'The drawing office squads were always sociable and quite often had nights out together. The draughtsmen's union DATA would hold 'smokers' social events where games of darts and dominoes were interspersed with the odd pint of beer or two.

'The people in the drawing office ran the car club treasure hunts, as well as the company's rugby team. They even produced their own hugely popular in-house magazine, *The Democritic*, which was a touch satirical.' This magazine was full of fun and humour and Ian says it was enjoyed by management and staff alike.

Les Hodgson, of Hadrian Park, worked at Swan's for 39 years, starting as an apprentice plater in 1953 and eventually becoming a head foreman. He was made redundant when the old company of Swan Hunter collapsed in 1993.

Derek Henderson

Wallsend residents and visitors turn out for the launch of the polar research ship James Clark Ross, left, in December 1990 at the Wallsend Yard. The ceremony was performed by the Queen. The large vessel on the right is the RFA Fort George, launched the following year.

Les remembers in c1953-54 seeing the last of the yard's ships to receive a substantial amount of riveting. 'This was done around the keel and at the aft end.' However, some riveting continued to be used in a small way in specific areas of ships as late as the 1960s.

It is clear Les took a great pride in his work, as did most men at the Wallsend Yard. A job which he particularly enjoyed was the destroyer HMS *Coventry*, completed in 1988. She was finished to a very high standard and the workers were praised for their efforts by the vessel's captain. 'In my opinion she was one of the best ships we had built,' says Les. During this period he was head foreman plater in charge of caulkers, burners and shipwrights as well as platers.

But his shipbuilding days have left him with pleural plaque, a medical condition produced by exposure to asbestos. This material, now known to be highly damaging to health, was used extensively to cover such items as engine casings, boilers and pipes aboard vessels.

Les was sometimes called upon to handle both blue and white asbestos and was often present when it was being sawn into shaped sections to fit around pipes and other installations. Asbestos dust would cover the decks. In the more safety-conscious 21st century, it is sometimes hard for us to understand why this material was used for so long.

Another hazard was welder's flash. This produced a burning sensation in the eyes. Les recalls that while working on the *Bergensfjord* he got too close to some aluminium welders and suffered

the effects of this flash. He went to the ambulance room to have drops put in his eyes to combat the problem.

Les has happy memories of the town's flourishing social scene when he was a young man. He has lived in Wallsend all his life. In the late 1950s and early 60s he went to dances regularly held on Saturday nights at Wallsend Memorial Hall. Many Swan's workers came to them. 'We jived to a superb jazz band. It was great fun. The hall must have had the best sprung dancing floor in the country.'

The building of the Memorial Hall at a cost of £15,000, was paid for by the directors and employees of Swan's as a

Wallsend Memorial Hall

The brand new Wallsend Memorial Hall c.1925 with its fine sprung dance floor. The glass roof was covered over in 1939 so that dances could go on during World War 2. The Memorial Hall still flourishes.

tribute to the company's workers who lost their lives in the First World War. It was opened in 1925.

A war memorial by North-East sculptor Roger Hedley, son of Victorian Newcastle artist Ralph Hedley, is a feature of the hall's exterior in Frank Street. It is flanked by the finely-modelled figures of a soldier and sailor. A relief above the names of those who fell, both in the First and Second world wars, depicts a warship on the sea. In the centre of the memorial another relief shows men in a shipyard workshop.

When industry boomed, so did the town. 'The High Street was full of people and the shops sold almost everything. You could buy a suit if you wanted. It was lined with pubs as well as shops. At one time we had five cinemas.'

In 1993 disaster engulfed the old Swan Hunter company when it failed to win the order for the helicopter carrier HMS *Ocean*. The business collapsed, the receivers were called in and wave after wave of mass redundancies followed. It was a hard time for Wallsenders and a low point in the fortunes of the district.

For two years the fate of the yard, and with it the fate of shipbuilding on the river, hung in the balance. Then, in 1995, only days before an auction of the Wallsend yard's equipment was due to take place, the Dutch-owned THC group purchased the yard for £5 million. A new company, Swan Hunter (Tyneside) Ltd., headed by Dutch businessman Jaap Kroese, was formed to operate the yard. Shipbuilding on the Tyne had been saved from extinction. At the time of writing the company is engaged on completing two amphibious landing ships, RFA *Largs Bay* and RFA *Lyme Bay*, and the new Swan's is on course to help build two large aircraft carriers for the Royal Navy.

The war memorial in Frank Street.

Looking back on the shipyard's proud history, it is the daily legion of workers pouring up and down Swan's Bank which remains indelibly imprinted in the memory. The peaceful endeavours of those hardworking men and women replaced the military might of the soldiers in the Roman legions who trod that same Wallsend earth so many years before.

Wallsend Timeline

AD120s Hadrian's Wall and Segedunum Roman Fort built.

c410 Roman occupation effectively at an end.

c1150 Holy Cross Church founded.

1781 The A Pit, the first shaft of Wallsend Colliery, begins production.

1807 St Peter's Church foundation stone laid.

1835 Wallsend Colliery Disaster in which 102 men and boys are killed.

1839 Steam railway opens between Newcastle and North Shields.

1854 Wallsend Colliery flooded. Production ceases.

1862 Wallsend Co-op founded.

1873 Wallsend Slipway & Engineering opens.

1879 Riverside Branch railway opens.

1874 Swan Hunter's Wallsend Shipyard founded.

1895 St Luke's Church foundation stone laid.

1897-98 Wallsend Colliery reopens with the new H Pit and old G Pit.

1904 First electric trains run on Newcastle-North Shields-Tynemouth loop line.

1906 The famous passenger liner *Mauretania* launched at Wallsend Shipyard.

1907 The *Mauretania* completed.

1908 Wallsend Town Hall in High Street opens.

1908 Rising Sun Colliery opens.

1909 The Borough Theatre opens.

1930s G, H and Edward pits close.

1957 New St Columba's RC Church consecrated.

1969 Supertanker *Esso Northumbria* launched at Wallsend Shipyard.

1969 Rising Sun Colliery closes.

1981 The Metro opens.

1993 Old Swan Hunter company collapses. Mass redundancies follow.

1994 Memorial plaque to colliery disaster victims unveiled in St Peter's Churchyard.

1995 New owner saves Swan's Wallsend Shipyard which becomes Swan Hunter (Tyneside) Ltd.

2000 Segedunum Roman Fort, Baths and Museum open to public.

Further reading

Folks alang the road, Alfred Senior (A. Senior, 1980)

History of Northumberland. Vol XIII, Madeleine Hope Dodds (Andrew Reid, 1930).

History of the Parish of Wallsend, William Richardson. (First published by Northumberland Press, Newcastle, 1923. New edition published by Newcastle Libraries & Information Service, and North Tyneside Libraries, 1998, reprinted 1999).

Images of England: Wallsend, Ken Hutchinson. (Tempus Publishing, 2005).

Swan Hunter – The Pride and the Tears, Ian Rae and Ken Smith (Tyne Bridge Publishing, 2001).

Swans of the Tyne: A Pictorial Tribute to the Achievements of Tyne Shipbuilders Swan Hunter, Ian Rae and Ken Smith (Newcastle City Libraries & Arts and North Tyneside Libraries, 1994).

Wallsend Colliery Pit Disaster 18th June 1835, Ken and Pauline Hutchinson. (Published by North Tyneside Libraries for Wallsend Local History Society, 1994).

Where the Wall Ends. (Wallsend Arts Centre, 1977).